SELMA LAGERLÖF'S
Words *of* Love *and* Wisdom

"God has more than one string to His bow."

Selected and edited by Joan Liffring-Zug Bourret

Associate editors: Greta Anderson,
Dorothy Crum and Melinda Bradnan

The Words of Wisdom Series

This book, *Selma Lagerlöf's Words of Love and Wisdom*, is third in a series featuring folk wisdom and excerpts from great works. The first title, *Proverbs of the North, Words of Wisdom from the Vikings*, was translated from the Icelandic by Joanne Asala, who earned a degree in English with emphasis on Medieval Literature from the University of Iowa.

The second title in this series is *Words of Wisdom and Magic from the Kalevala* translated by Richard Impola. With a Ph.D. in English Literature, he retired from college teaching to pursue a second career as a translator. The *Kalevala* is a compilation of Finnish oral poetry dating back hundreds of years. On February 28, 1835, Elias Lönnrot signed his name to the *Foreword of the Kalevala* or *Old Poems of Karelia from the Ancient Times of the Finnish People*.

The Selma Lagerlöf Series

With most of her work out of print for over half a century, Nobel Prize winning author Selma Lagerlöf's fiction has gone unnoticed by recent generations of readers. This series, complete with chronologies, notes, and illustrations, seeks to perpetuate her work—captivating, timeless classics in their themes and expression.

Acknowledgements
Graphic design: Robyn Loughran and Molly Cook, M.A. Cook Design

Books by Mail
For a complete list of all titles available please contact:
Penfield Press, 215 Brown Street, Iowa City, Iowa 52245
Penfield Press http://www.penfield-press.com

© Penfield Press
ISBN 1-57216-032-2
Library of Congress 00 131061

Introduction

The profound truth that comes across in Selma Lagerlöf's stories is the fact that people do not act according to opinions or principles, but are driven by inner irrational forces. Thus, in all our confrontations in life, our actions are always unpredictable.

Together with August Strindberg (1849–1912), Selma Lagerlöf (1858–1940) is probably the most well-known literary figure to have come out of Sweden. During her lifetime her stories and novels were read and enjoyed all over the world, particularly after she became the first woman to receive the prestigious Nobel Prize for Literature in 1909. Her works have powerful imagery and themes that make them universal and timeless. Also, as an avid supporter of causes such as women's rights and world peace, her thoughts and concerns are equally valid today.

Selma Lagerlöf was born in the ancestral manor home of Mårbacka, in the province of Värmland in Sweden. Her childhood was marked by an illness that forced her to avoid strenuous activities, but which opened up a world of stories and books instead. Of particular importance to her development as an author was the abundance of family legends and regional tales that her grandmother passed on to her, as well as the rich tradition of Nordic stories and mythology that surrounded her.

Lagerlöf was a schoolteacher and wrote fiction on the side for ten years before she was able to support herself solely with her writing. Her first novel, *Gösta Berling's Saga* published in 1891, did not immediately get the enthusiastic reception it deserved.

— John Lofgren, Ph.D.

Dr. John Lofgren is Director of the Center For The Arts, Vero Beach, Florida. Born in Sweden, he studied in the United States receiving a Ph.D. in art history from the University of Oregon. In 1987, he was named officer of the Royal Order of the Polar Star, bestowed by the King of Sweden.

Chronology

1858	Selma Lagerlöf born November 20 at Mårbacka in Värmland, Sweden.
1863	Grandmother Lisa Maja Lagerlöf dies.
1867	Visits Stockholm for treatment of lameness.
1873	Second visit to Stockholm, wrote *The Stockholm Diary*.
1882–1885	Studies at a teachers' college for gifted women in Stockholm.
1885	Father dies.
1885–1895	Works as a teacher at a junior high school for girls at Landskrona in southern Sweden.
1888	Mårbacka sold.
1891	First novel, *Gösta Berling's Saga*, published.
1894	*Invisible Links*, a collection of stories.
1895–1896	Travel in Italy and Europe, stipend from King Oscar II.
1897	Moves to Falun in the province of Dalecarlia.
1899	*Queens at Kungahälla*, stories about Scandinavian nobility.
1899–1900	Travel in Egypt and Israel.
1906–1907	*The Wonderful Adventures of Nils* and *The Further Adventures of Nils*, books originally commissioned by the government to teach schoolchildren Sweden's geography.
1907	Aunt Lovisa dies. Selma Lagerlöf purchases Mårbacka.
1908	*The Girl from the Marsh Croft*, stories.
1909	Wins the Nobel Prize for Literature.
1910	Becomes an active landowner at Mårbacka and lives there summers.
1914	Becomes a member of the Swedish Academy.
1919	Begins to live year-round at Mårbacka.
1922	*Mårbacka*, first part of her memoirs.
1930	*Memories of My Childhood*.
1932	*The Diary of Selma Lagerlöf*.
1934	*Harvest*, a selection of short prose.
1940	Dies, March 16.

Contents

Words of Love 7

Life's Pathways 13

Life's Tapestry 21

Swedish Homecoming 27

Moods of Nature 33

Fields of Strife 41

Old Songs 46

Words of Wisdom 49

Words *of* Love

Sunshine is like **love**.
Who does not know the misdeeds it has done,
and who can refuse to forgive it?
Gösta Berling's Saga

There is no bed so soft that it can give
comfort to one who is longing.
The Tale of a Manor

Love is an illness, but it is not mortal.
"A Fallen King"

from *Gösta Berling's Saga*

Joy held the reins,
   and Youth and Beauty
      stood on the runners.

The heart is incorrigible in its habit of loving.
For every sorrow caused by **love**,
it knows no other cure than a newer **love**,
as those who have burned themselves
with a hot iron deaden the pain by
burning themselves once more.

Why should love only be healed by
LOVE?

Better unhappiness with **Love**
than happiness without it.

Is your heart so great that it can conquer itself and smile?

Gossip is not very merciful toward young women.

Love is strong when it has gone through the fire of pain.

Love lives by **love**, and not by service and good works.

A man unmarried has no sorrow.

*She always prayed to God to preserve her from **love**.*

The uneasy heart is forever going astray; evil makes the evil worse.

Love invariably leads us aright. But it takes great courage and faith to obey its promptings. . . .

Can any bliss be likened to stolen happiness?

But if he loved her, why did he not remember that he could give her no worse gift than his **love**?

Love would lend fire to his words.

A woman does not wish to feel ashamed of a man she has **loved**.

 from *The Tale of a Manor*

Love could not be shown
in words, but had to be shown
every day
and every hour
as long as life
lasted.

Loving takes the perfume from the roses,
 and the light from the new moon. . . .

There is an old song:
 "Old husband in the cottage,
 young lover in the wood,
 wife who runs away,
 child who cries,
 home without a mistress."
The song is often sung.
Everybody understands it.
 "A Fallen King"

Strange beings these husbands.
They beat us; they drink up our money;
they pawn our furniture.
Why on earth had our Lord created them?
"A Fallen King"

*There are other things fire can do
besides give light and warmth
and cook the food. What awakens
a thirst for pleasure in the man's
soul but a flame? It flickers in
and around the body of a man
as does the flame
around the rough log.*
The General's Ring

Life's Pathways

For a moment, dreaming and reality seemed to her to be standing side by side as rivals. . . . Dreaming stood sunnily smiling and showering life's happiness upon her. But coarse, hard life came with a little mite of friendliness to show that it did not mean so badly by her as had seemed.

The Tale of a Manor

Nothing of youth played in her veins. She was born old.

"A Fallen King"

 **from *Gösta Berling's Saga***

The only reason for which a fête is worth giving is that eyes might shine, and hearts and feet might dance, and joy might again find a place among mankind. . . .Old men and women become young again and laugh and rejoice.

Friends, children of men!
You who dance and you who laugh,
I pray that you dance carefully
and laugh kindly, for much sorrow may
come to pass if your thin-soled,
silken shoe treads upon a
tender human heart instead of
hard floor planks, and your gay,
silver-ringing laugh may drive a
soul to despair.

In the lottery of life, she had drawn music, dancing, and adventure.

She would like the world to be quite level, without any stones or hills or lakes, so that you could dance over it all. She would like to dance all the way from her cradle to her grave. . . .

He who cannot lift his foot to dance,
nor open his mouth to laughter,
he is old;
he feels the atrocious burden of years.

Old butterflies ought to die while the sun shines.

The pastor says to the thief, "Do not steal!" and
to the evil man, "You must not beat your wife,"
and to the cripple, "You must believe in God
and not in the devil and in goblins!"
But the thief answers, "Give me bread!"
and the evil man answers, "Make us rich,
and we will not quarrel," and the cripple says,
"Teach me better."

Who of us sails securely?
Round us surges sorrow like a
foaming sea; see how its waves
hungrily lick the sides of the vessel;
see how they try to board her!
Oh, there is no sure anchorage,
no firm ground, no trusty ship,
as far as the eye can reach,
only an unknown heaven over the
sea of trouble.

Death is life's wage.

Death, pale friend,
my strength against yours is weakness,
but I tell you that your fight was harder
against the women of the olden days. . . .
no cold could cool their fiery blood.

People often persecute others trying to save their own souls.

Dreary are the paths men tread on earth, over desert and marsh and mountain. *Must the outcast go the way of the outcasts?* The way of anger and trouble and unhappiness? What does it matter if he stumbles and falls? Is there any one to restrain him? Is there any one who would stretch out to him a supporting hand, or offer him a pleasant drink? *Where are the fairy princesses who should strew roses over the dreary paths?*

The soul is ever hungering. It cannot live on vanity and frivolity alone.

The spirit of self-analysis —
with icy eyes and long knotted fingers —
sits in the darkest corner of our souls
and plucks our being to pieces as old
women pluck scraps of wool and silk.
Piece by piece, the long, hard fingers
have dissected us till our whole being
lies there like a heap of rags —
till all our best feelings, our innermost
thoughts, all we have said and done are
examined and ransacked, disintegrated,
and the icy eyes have watched,
and the toothless mouth has sneered
and whispered, "See, it is but rags,
nothing but rags."

Young horses who cannot bear the whip or spur find life hard. At every smart they start forward and rush to their destruction, and when the way is stony and difficult, they know no better expedient than to overturn the cart and gallop madly away.

Is there any use in bewailing that the sun sinks every evening in the west and leaves the world in darkness? Who is invincible without submissiveness? Who can conquer without patience?

We are only fuel

    enveloped by the fires of life,

whose sparks fly

    from one to the other.

    We ignite,

        flame up,

            and die out.

Life's Tapestry

He fancied he saw before him his own life and the life of the people whom he had known, and with whom he had lived, forming a small portion of God's great weaving, and he seemed to see that piece so distinctly that he could discern both outlines and coloring. . . .he would be obliged to confess that it was the life of himself and his friends which he wove into the rug as a faint imitation of what he thought he had seen represented on God's loom.

"A Story from Halstanäs"

The kingdom is better served with men than with money. . . .
"The Silver Mine"

We all know, without doubt, the kind of faces which we find not at all remarkable until we get a chance to see them in the moment of some great happiness or in the midst of a roguish prank or, perhaps best of all, when their owners are confronted with something difficult or trying.
"The Natural Beauty of Värmland"

He wished to have his grief again so that he might speak. He was a painter without hands, a singer who had lost his voice. He had only spoken of his sorrow. What should he speak of now?
"A Fallen King"

from *Gösta Berling's Saga*

The truth of the matter was that the organist had only two cows, but he called one Twelve and the other Eleven, so that it should sound grand when he talked of them.

He was so obstinate that if he had stood in the midst of the fires of hell, and had seen all the devils grinning at him, he would still have said they were not there. . . .

Oh, you wild birds, you fly daringly, but the Lord knows the net that will catch you.

He knew well that joy was a blessing to the children of men, and that it must exist, but like a great mystery, the question hung over the world. . . . how a man was both to be joyous and good. He said it was the easiest and most difficult of things.

There is so much trouble among the poor which a kind hand and a warm heart can lighten.

Great will be my fame if the poor care to remember me a few years after my death. I shall have done sufficient good if I have planted a couple of apple trees at the house corners, if I have taught the village fiddlers a few of the old master's melodies, and if the shepherd boy learns a few new songs to sing in the forest paths.

Lady Musica is the very best company for those who are suffering. She is gay and playful as a child; she is fiery and engaging as a young woman, and good and wise as the old who have lived a righteous life.

What has the spirit to do with temples of clay and stone? Learn to build everlasting castles of dreams and visions!

To **weave** is a comfort for all sorrow, it absorbs all other interests, and has been the saving of many a woman.

It was only poverty that made her so strangely harsh.
The Tale of a Manor

There must be both light and dark shades in the weaving.
Girl from the Marsh Croft

There was just enough work and just enough play, and every day there was another reason to be happy.
The Further Adventures of Nils

The meek in the land shall raise their heads and think that, after all, it is they who have chosen the better part.
"Addresses"

Swedish Homecoming

St. Birgitta came to the land of Sweden with her message in the midst of a century of pest, internal strife, and weakness. Did she evoke the courage that saved liberty? Did the thought that this honest Swedish woman had been one of their own give the necessary encouragement to make the people realize their own worth and strength?

Harvest: Swedish Legends and Recollections

 from *The Wonderful Adventures of Nils*

The plain could have been the homespun cloth. . . .the people decorated it with cities and farms, churches and factories, castles and railway stations. Roofs shone like trinkets in the morning light, and windowpanes glittered like jewels. . . . the country gardens were like little brooches and buttons.

Småland is a tall house with spruce trees on the roof, and leading up to it is a broad stairway with three big steps, and this stairway is called Blekinge. It stretches forty-two miles along the frontage of Småland house. Anyone who would like to go all the way down to the East Sea, by way of the stairs, has twenty-four miles to walk.

This island is actually a butterfly longing for its wings.

from *Gösta Berling's Saga*

There was nothing wonderful about it — there was no lake, no waterfall, no shores nor park, but, for all that, it was beautiful because it was a good and peaceful home. . . . Things that, in other places, would have brought forth bitterness and anger were here smoothed away so mildly. Thus it should be in a true home.

Many have seen the home of their childhood return their gaze like a wounded animal.

No place on earth is so wretched to enter upon as a ruined home.

What will become of this whole blessed house, where everything except work thrives so contentedly?

May life be like a rosebush, with flowers of love, wind, and pleasure, and may its roses hang within every man's reach; that is our heart's desire, and our land wears the features of sternness and renunciation. *Our land is the symbol of perpetual meditation, but we have no thoughts!*

You should see the Löfven on an early summer morning when it lies wide awake under its veil of mist. . . .It seems as if it would coquette with you at first, so gently, so gradually does it creep out of its light covering, and so enchantingly beautiful is it that you hardly recognize it till suddenly it flings its veil aside and lies there naked and rosy, glittering in the sunshine. . . .But it is not content with a life of pleasure alone. . . .It is often in an angry mood and turning white with sudden fury, wrecks the sailing boats, but it can also lie in dreamy quiet and reflect the sky.

To describe the country is a task that defies the power of one who can only wield the pen.

 **from "The Natural Beauty of Värmland"**

The sun made short shrift with the mist, scattering it in all directions, leaving only enough to make a much needed veil of beauty for this poor country.

The country appeared so slumberingly still. It seemed as if all Swedish life wanted to find its way up here to lie down in peace and thoroughly rest up.

Up here passes a border between two countries. *Perhaps there also passes a border of another kind. A border that divides the visible from the invisible, the real from the unreal.*

You come across stunted ridges which have never reached their full height. You would more than like to seize them by their bent necks and lift them aloft a bit. They are broad enough, strong enough; they could very well allow themselves to rise a little more boldly to the sky.

For how much did I have to thank this old homestead? It looked at me with questioning and reproach. "What would you be without me? Why don't you come and take care of me now when I need you?"

Memories of Mårbacka

Only those who labor forever with the soil can hold this land in good repute.

The Wonderful Adventures of Nils

Moods *of* Nature

One who lies still in a brook and never hears anything new can't know very much.

"The Musician"

from *Gösta Berling's Saga*

You who guard the fields and meadows and parks and the happy flower gardens — *guard them well! With love and work!* It is not well that Nature should sorrow over mankind.

How much quieter are the bright sunny days than the dark nights, under whose sheltering wing the wild beasts hunt and the owls hoot!

She saw the strife of day and night, and how everything living seemed to fear it. Horses hurried forward the last load to gain their stables as quickly as possible; the woodcutters hurried home from the forest — the dairymaids from the farmyard. Wild beasts howled in the forest clearing.

The promised land flows with
milk and honey. We empty the
mountains of their iron, and fill
our cellars with wine. The fields bear
gold with which we gild life's misery,
and we fell our forests to build
pavilions and skittle alleys.

Trust not the brook with its sweet waters!
It has sickness and death for you. . . . Trust not
the cuckoo which calls so joyfully in spring.
In autumn it changes into a hawk with
cruel eyes and awful claws.

The fair sun is like a mother whose son
 is about to set off for a far-off land,
and who, in the hour of the leave-taking,
cannot take her eyes from the beloved.
The plain, which is good and fertile
and loves cultivation, wages constant
**war against the hills. The plain
laments its want of room —
and that it has no view.**

I would be friends with the clear air that trembles over the blue mountains and with the glittering sun and the beautiful stars, for it often seems to me that dead things feel and suffer with the living — the gulf between us is not so wide as we imagine.

The spirit of life still lives in dead things.

The bees were as large as geese and the beehives? Just like our own beehives. How did the bees get into them? That was their own affair. The giant bees of Fancy have thronged about us. . .how they are to enter the beehives of Reality is surely their own affair!

When the little bee came again, its humming was like a hum to life. "Oh, thou beauteous life," it said, "I thank thee that happy work among roses and sunshine has fallen to my lot. I thank thee that I can enjoy thee without anxiety or fear. Well I know that spiders lie in wait and beetles steal, but happy work is mine, and brave freedom from care. Oh, thou beauteous life, thou glorious existence!"
"Among the Climbing Roses"

May the old legends swarm round you like summer bees.
Gösta Berling's Saga

Let her tramp upon gray stone streets; let her live in cramped city rooms with no other outlook than gray stone walls; let her live among people who hide everything that is unusual in them and who appear to be all alike. It may, perchance, teach her to see that which is waiting outside the gate of her home — all that lives and moves between the stretch of blue hills which she has every day before her eyes.
"The Story of a Story"

from *The Tale of a Manor*

One ought to take up and kiss the first sod whose grass appeared above the snow. One should pick the first nettle leaf merely to burn one's skin because it was now spring.

Nothing is so certain as that the sun loves the open spaces outside the small country churches. . . . nowhere else do the sunbeams weave such a dense net of light; nowhere else does the atmosphere hold such a solemn stillness.

If there is nothing else that flourishes in a garden, it affords good soil for dreams.

from *The Wonderful Adventures of Nils*

The water had reflected the sky so perfectly that it had become one with the sky. . . . What was up and what was down, what was east and what was west, he had no way of knowing.

The hillside begins to adorn itself. . . . It no longer cares about pines and spruce, but casts them off like old, everyday clothes, and parades later with big oaks and lindens and chestnuts, and with blossoming leafy bowers, and becomes as gorgeous as a manor park. And when it meets the sea, the hillside is so changed it doesn't know itself.

Nils had never understood the real meaning of "night." It was as if the whole world had become petrified and would never come to life again.

Where the land leans toward the sea, it raises a wall of hills in front of it, as though the sea were dangerous.

The foxes had thrown themselves on the sheep just for sport — just to hunt them and tear them to death.

Fields *of* Strife

It was then that a very great and holy night sank down over the earth. It was the darkest night that any one had ever seen. One could have believed that the whole earth had fallen into a cellar-vault. It was impossible to distinguish water from land, and one could not find one's way on the most familiar road. And it couldn't be otherwise, for not a ray of light came from heaven. All the stars stayed at home in their own houses, and the fair moon held her face averted.

Christ Legends

from *Gösta Berling's Saga*

More die in the flight than on the field of battle.

He had fought like a good soldier. . . . He felt all Nature hated him because he had taken a part in such things. Those possessing wider knowledge could comfort themselves with the idea of having fought for their country and its honor. What did he know of such things?

The horror of war broke over the land. . . . He came home again without a wound or any damaged limb, but he had received a scar for life. . . .He had seen too much of the wickedness of the world and man's cruelty to man; he no longer saw kindness anywhere.

He who lives in the forest must acquire happy memories, or he sees nothing but murder and persecution among plants and animals, as he saw before among men.

The beasts of the forest were now his enemies; so were the hills which hid the sun, and the marsh which sent forth the cold mist. The forest is a dreadful home for those who cherish evil thoughts.

Life and nature are hard. They bring forth courage and joy as a counterweight against their own hardness, or no one could endure them.

Silence, you who croak of misfortune! Wait till night, if you would hoot in concert with the forest owl.

When hate and war fill the world,
everything must suffer.
Then the ocean becomes wild
and rapacious as a robber,
and the fields are as hard and
unyielding as a miser.

*He only wanted someone to fight
with, now that he had a weapon.*

It seemed that to those who saw nothing but want and misery before them it was a pleasure to hit at something — it did not matter who it was or what they hit. As soon as the strong and pugnacious saw that a fight was going on, they rushed in from all sides.

The times were such that the good often brought as much ruin as the evil.

I shall live here in fear and trembling, knowing that all I do leads to sorrow and sin, knowing that in helping one, I am harming another.

The mother cried out in despair,
"Happy they who mourn their dead with tears!
I must stand dry-eyed at the grave of my son;
I must rejoice over his death.
What unhappiness is mine!"

The falcon will never be able to overcome the owl. Only a dove can do that, only a dove.

Old Songs

Trust not in happiness, trust not in the expression of happiness, nor in roses and dewy leaves.

Trust not in the dance. Many feet swing lightly over polished floors, while the mind is as heavy as lead.

Trust not in a laugh.

Trust not in the jest, for many go to table with jesting lips while ready to die of sorrow.

The sad heart is easily tempted to smiles, but he who is happy cannot weep.

The old songs believe only in tears, in sadness. Sorrow is the reality, the imperishable, it is the firm rock under the shifting sand. One can trust in sorrow and sorrow's symbols.

The turtle-dove drinks clear water, but always muddies it first with its foot to better suit its pensive mind. So life pleases more when touched with melancholy.

His sorrow seemed to her to borrow all voices, to make itself masks of everything it met.
"A Fallen King"

You only imagine that your suffering is the hardest on earth. But there are others who have it worse than you.
The Tale of a Manor

Next time I get into trouble, I'll remember and bear in mind that there's never a reason to harm myself or others.

There is always a third way out if you can hit upon it.

The Further Adventures of Nils

Words *of* Wisdom

He who has not spoken at the right time may have to repent it a whole lifetime.
"A Fallen King"

There is much to be endured if one reads the whole Bible when only ten years old!
"The Vow"

from *Gösta Berling's Saga*

One does not ask leave of the fox to take his skin.

**What is the grief of youth?
It still has strength and hope.**

You who are loved by heaven and earth should not increase the burden of those whom heaven and earth despise.

She neither loved nor hated. . . .
she understood them all.
She that understands does not hate.

May you ever be mistress of your own tongue and your own hand when anger fills your soul.

There is no great difficulty in waiting when you are sure of your object, and when there is much to engage your thoughts.

God's storm forgets no one; it overwhelms the great and the small.

There is a suffering of the soul that outweighs all the pains of the body.

When men are silent, the stones bear witness.

It is possible to be joyous when you don't know sorrow and only hear it mentioned as a guest in another country.

A hero is created of different clay from other men.

The drink

is a fur covering in winter and
a cooling draught in summer.
It means a warm hut
and a soft bed.

No outer brilliance nor great talent
made this man so highly honored
— it was because he always kept
in God's path.

    Who can be safer than she whom
          God must Himself guard?
    You must not dream of having been
    sent by God — everybody is that,
                    you know.

Oh! do not make me rich.
Do not lay such duties upon me.

It is marvelous that feeble humanity can withstand so much persecution.

Teach us that although our bodies have grown heavy and our joints stiff, in our feelings we are ever the same.

It is often the case with the silent children about us, that they cherish a dream which they dare not talk about.

She held views of her own about many things, as is apt to be the case with those who sit much alone and let their thoughts dwell on what their eyes have seen.

Hard truth can come wrapped in happy memories, in feelings of regret and gratitude.

What is the good in being a master — aye, even the greatest of masters — if one cannot duplicate one's inventions for the benefit of mankind?

Who in our time complains of having received too much from the Goddess Genius?

from *The Tale of a Manor*

Sometimes one encounters events which take the air of symbols and signs requiring interpretation.

If she had not formed hopes, she would not have felt such a terrible disappointment.

They had no standard by which to gauge reality, therefore they were inaccessible to its sharp edge.

from *The Further Adventures of Nils*

It's better to keep a firm hold upon one's purse and be called stingy, than to be in debt like other farm owners.

Do the wild geese intend to dress up in wild feathers?
Do they think that makes swans of them?

The more you put into your heads, the more you can get into them.

Because he had always been self-centered, he was not lonely for anyone he used to know.

The Wonderful Adventures of Nils

While their mother was ill,
she had often told them that
she never regretted having let
the sick woman stay with them.
It was not hard to die when
one had done right, she said,
for then one could leave
this life with a clear
conscience.

The Further Adventures of Nils

"If you have learned anything at all from us, Thumbietot, you no longer think the humans should have the whole earth to themselves," the wild goose said solemnly. "Remember you have a large country and you can easily afford to leave a few bare rocks, a few shallow lakes and swamps, a few desolate cliffs and remote forests to us poor, dumb creatures, where we can be allowed to live in peace. All my days I have been hounded and hunted. It would be a comfort to know that there is a refuge somewhere for one like me.

The Further Adventures of Nils

Works by Selma Lagerlöf

Christ Legends
The Emperor of Portugallia
Girl from the Marsh Croft
Gösta Berling's Saga
Harvest
Jerusalem
Liliecrona's Home
Miracles of the Antichrist
Queens of Kungahälla and Other Sketches
The Ring of the Löwenskölds
The Tale of a Manor
The Treasure

Autobiographical writings
  Mårbacka
  Memories of My Childhood:
    Further Years at Mårbacka
  The Diary of Selma Lagerlöf

Children's stories
  The Wonderful Adventures of Nils
  The Further Adventures of Nils